Dropshipping

The complete dropshipping guide, teaching you how to make money online!

Table of Contents

Introduction 1

Chapter 1: Opening Your Online Store 2

Chapter 2: Understanding Dropshipping and How It Works 11

Chapter 3: The Benefits of Dropshipping 17

Chapter 4: Manufacturers vs. Dropship Wholesaler 20

Chapter 5: Using Shopify for Dropshipping 22

Chapter 6: AliExpress Dropshipping 26

Chapter 7: Finding Products to Sell 28

Conclusion 31

Introduction

Thank you for taking the time to pick up this book about dropshipping!

Dropshipping is a business model that is rapidly growing in popularity, and for good reason. Dropshipping allows absolutely anyone to start an online business with very low up-front cost. This can also be done from anywhere with an internet connection, allowing the dropshipper to operate independent of a physical location!

Whether you're new to business, or just looking to expand your current business, this book aims to help you become a profitable dropshipper in no time!

Once again, thanks for choosing this book, I hope you find it to be helpful!

Chapter 1: Opening Your Online Store

The evolution of technology in the last fifteen years has had a dramatic effect on the way people do business. Because of this, people from across all industries have taken their businesses online - creating a new avenue of opportunities for people who would like to change the way they see business. An online business presence creates huge opportunities with advertising, marketing, management, and the overall processes of the business, because it opens up the shop to people from all over the world. As a matter of fact, recent research concluded that shopping on the internet is still growing, with a whopping fifty-one percent of Americans preferring to shop online instead of the traditional way.

To add, research studies show that online businesses reached a total sales volume of $202 billion in 2015, and $320 billion in the year 2016. With this much cash on the table, you may be one of those who are considering taking the leap and building your business on the web. Luckily, this book's objective is to help you understand the rules of the game and give you all the information you require to start and grow your online business.

In case you're one of those entrepreneurs who don't have an online store yet, we have a truckload of reasons why you should get started! Here are a few of those reasons:

1. **It Helps Develop Your Client Base**

    A physical store caters to people within the premises of your locality. That's one of the biggest differences with an online store, because it can be accessed by anybody – any place on the planet. Furthermore, it's also easier to spread the word online amongst individuals, and gain a following for your brand.

2. **It Can Give You More Control Over Your Business**

    An online store can give you more control over your business through areas such as advertising, marketing, and sales. It likewise gives you a more prominent level of adaptability with your stock, even if you don't have the items on hand.

3. **It Keeps Your Business Aggressive**

    With the current technology offered today, more and more people are going online for their purchases. What's more is that they can easily discover anything on the web. If your business doesn't have an online store, it would be simple for even your most faithful clients to purchase from competition on the off chance that they didn't have the time or the need to visit your physical store.

4. It Obliges Your Clients

One of the greatest aces of e-commerce is that buyers can shop at whatever point they would like, day in and day out, even on times outside regular hours. You should note that clients have become used to getting what they need, when they need it, and that your business should be the first to offer a correspondingly helpful service online.

5. It Can Bring Down Your Overhead

Now this can be a good thing and a bad thing. A bad thing for your employees since you will be freeing up irrelevant positions, but it's a good thing for your business. In case you're simply starting your business, opting for an online store (in comparison to a physical store) can help bring down your underlying and continuous overhead. An online store likely requires far less staff to begin with, and you may not have to put resources into building stock, especially if you use a dropshipping model like this book will later talk about.

6. Your Earnings Keep Coming In

Talk about earning day in and day out. Since your online store is open 24 hours a day, 7 days a week, this also means you have a great chance of earning profit while you sleep!

Initial Steps to Start Your Online Store

When you begin constructing your store, initial steps include brainstorming on how you'd like your online store to look, your target market, as well as the look and feel of your shop. You'll need to consider the layout of your website, and start setting up your essential pages, including your profile and marketplace, home page and brand page, and anything else that you feel is essential to your brand.

Choose Your Online Store Host

An initial step of any online business is picking the correct platform to assemble your webpage on. There's no "perfect" site to host your online store – it basically comes down to your individual preferences which help you figure you out which site will serve you best.

There are a lot of online store hosting platforms out there and picking the best one for you will be a breeze especially if you know what you are looking for. Shopify and WooCommerce are two popular examples. Compare options, and choose what will be easiest for you to use and navigate, while also having your customer in mind!

Pick Your Store's Name

You need to pick a web address for your site. Your domain is the web address where clients locate your online store. This is a major business choice, so don't trifle with it. In the event that you can, pick a name that is short, basic, and depicts your business. Try to make it easy to remember, so that your shop will be the first thing that comes to mind when customers think of a particular item.

Choose an Arrangement

Open source: Open source arrangements are usually free downloads that expect you to construct your site with no help. While this is an awesome decision for full customization, expect to encounter some overwhelming programming when designing the site - which may mean you'll have to procure somebody to help you set up your online shop.

Facilitated: Hosted arrangements house your site on their servers, and additionally give electronic programming to fabricate and control your online store. This option is most appropriate for novices in site building.

Marketing Your Business

Once your site is prepared for the world to see, you have to drive clients to your store with advertising. Regardless of whether you use email, Facebook ads, SEO, or other different types of web based advertising, it's important that you share your store with the majority. As it were, regardless of whether you have the most astounding site on the planet, if nobody can discover your store, you'll battle to make any money.

Set Up Your Payment Portal

We're all in business to profit, right? In that case, you'll need to figure out how exactly you'll process and collect payments from your customers. Some startup entrepreneurs start off with PayPal or Google Checkout, as they are quite simple to add to most websites. Another increasingly popular option is called Stripe. Compare the options that suit you best, keeping in mind that some services such as Shopify are often already integrated with payment processors, which will make the process all that much easier for you.

Finding Your Niche

Before you do anything, it's imperative to choose what sorts of products you'll offer on the web. Whatever you pick, it's usually a good idea to work with items that you're enthusiastic about. Odds are you'll be working with these items for a long while, so ensure it's something that won't effectively bore you later on. Once you've chosen which products to offer, there are a few parts of your online business that you will need to asses before you begin the construction of your webpage.

One key step when setting up your store is deciding on your specialty. What exactly is it that you'd like to sell? What problem are you solving by providing that product to your customers?

When deciding on what niche of products to sell, you might like to ask yourself the following questions:

- What are the things or items that you are enthusiastic about?

- What customer rejections might arise, and how can you respond to these?

- Is your product or service difficult to market or brand?

- In the event that you have a physical store, will you offer similar things that you offer in your store, or only a subset of your stock? Or on the other hand will you offer something totally extraordinary that is more suited to e-commerce?

Experience

When you have fully decided to open your business and take it online, you have to center around your customer's experience with your product or service. It's essential to have various photographs for every item on your site alongside product descriptions.

Transportation

When you start your business, one of the biggest things to consider is transportation, including shipment. One of the greatest concerns regarding shipment is the measurements and the weight of every item. The greater and heavier the item, the more expensive it will be to dispatch. Before launching your site, ensure that you have gathered accurate postage costs from your suppliers for each product, and to each area you will be selling to.

Business Costs

You will also need to ask yourself how much you are willing to spend to launch, run, and grow your business. How much will materials cost? What will your margins be? How much money are you willing to invest in advertising?

Sourcing

In the dropshipping model, you don't purchase any physical stock, until a purchase has been made. When someone orders the product from your website, you will then order it from your supplier, and provide them with the shipping address of the end customer. You never handle the stock, and simply keep the difference between what you charged the customer, and what the supplier charged you. That's your profit.

Obviously, drop shipping accompanies its own difficulties. Long supply chains can diminish net revenues, in case you're not watchful. And afterward there can be issues with providers and transporting, as well as stock availability. Whatever sourcing and conveyancing process you pick, ensure you completely measure the advantages and disadvantages.

Dropshipping is rapidly growing in popularity and acceptance, and many suppliers will already have experience with dropshippers. Terms will be different with every company, and some might even be reluctant to work with dropshippers. It's your job to get them on the phone, convince them that your business is worthwhile dealing with, and get a contract started!

Chapter 2: Understanding Dropshipping and How It Works

So what is exactly is dropshipping? Well, to explain in a simple way, dropshipping is a process that sets you up as the go between or the middle man between clients and providers.

In a broader way of explaining, dropshipping is a retail satisfaction strategy where a store doesn't keep the items it offers in stock. Rather, when a store offers an item, it buys the product from an outsider and has it transported straightforwardly to the client. Subsequently, the seller never observes or handles the item. The greatest contrast amongst dropshipping and the standard retail model is that the offering trader doesn't hold any stock. Rather, the seller only purchases the stock when a sale occurs on their site. This means that there are very low start-up costs associated with the dropshipping model.

Dropshipping isn't always perfect though. The model can have various inherent complexities and issues you'll quite possibly encounter.

We'll be looking at these issues and how to best address them in this chapter. Fortunately, with some watchful arranging and thought, the greater part of these issues can be overcome quite simply!

First of all, dropshipping is a method where you send your client's requests to producers or distributor and they send the items straightforwardly to your client. To put it simply, here are 3 basic steps of dropshipping.

1. Your customer purchases a product from your online store.

2. You purchase the product at wholesale price from your supplier, providing them with your customer's shipping information.

3. The provider sends the product directly to your customer.

Dropshipping is a great business model for many people, but for others it simply might not suit. Here are a few of the people that dropshipping is ideal for:

Individuals Who Are Concerned About Costs

Dropshipping is a very low cost way to get started with e-commerce. Because you don't need to purchase stock up front, you simply need to cover the cost of building your website, and advertising!

Individuals needing to test the market

Before diving head first into a business, it's a good idea to test the market. You'll want to test if there is actually a demand out there for the products you'd like to offer. Dropshipping is a great tool for this because it doesn't require you to have an inventory of items to begin with.

Individuals who'd like Diversity in Products

Dropshipping allows you to sell a wide variety of products, from a number of different brands. In order to add more products to your site, you'll simply need to create an arrangement with additional suppliers.

First Time Venders

Dropshipping is great for people who have never run an online store, yet want to give it a shot. It's a great, low-speculation approach to trying your hand at business. Dropshipping will give you a chance to test your sales skills, and hone your entrepreneurial prowess before having to deal with a fully-fledged store.

Tips for Your Dropshipping Store

Let's say you have set up your online store and you're ready to introduce a fresh, new experience to your current client base. All things considered, here are some tips on how to make sure your dropshipping endeavors become fully sustainable:

Select Your Products Wisely

This is the core of your dropshipping business, and numerous dropshippers all over the world have their own specific methods for picking items. One of the best places to do your research is to search on Dropship Directories online. Some sites include eBay, Shopify, Oberloo, AliExpress, and SalesHoo.

One of the other ways to do it is through contacting wholesalers directly. This can be more work, but it usually pays off and results in greater margins.

Go on the Digital Marketing Train

The more traffic you have, the more products you'll sell. Advertising is a key aspect when attracting customers, so don't hold back here. Having a blog on your website is a good idea, as it can draw in potential customers, as well as enhance your webpage's Search Engine Optimization (SEO). Investing in advertising on other websites such as Facebook, Google, and

YouTube is also a great idea. These websites get a huge amount of traffic, so having your ads show up in these places can really take your business to the next level!

Polish Your E-Commerce Store

Your site configuration will specifically influence sales. Test out different layouts, product images, descriptions, and discount deals. Tweak your website regularly to optimize it for sales.

Use Site Analytics

A web based business administrator's work is never done. Once your site is up and running, you'll have access to some analytics. You'll be able to see how many visitors each particular page gathers. With certain website apps and plugins you'll be able to gather even more information, such as how long people spend on each page, what items they add to cart, and during which steps of the checkout process that they abandon their cart. All of this information can help you to tweak and optimize your website, as well as your advertising to maximize both sales and profit margins.

Sample Scenario

To give you further insight into how dropshipping works, here is a sample scenario of what could transpire during the process of dropshipping.

1. Customer Places Order Online
2. E-Commerce Website Places The Order With The Supplier
3. Wholesaler Dropships The Order
4. E-Commerce Website Alerts Customer Of The Shipment

The turnaround time on dropshipped items is regularly speedier than you'd suspect. Most quality providers will have the capacity to get products packaged and posted within hours. If you are sourcing products from overseas, such as from AliExpress for example, it's a good idea to alert customers that they can expect slower shipping times.

Chapter 3: The Benefits of Dropshipping

If you think that dropshipping is the solution to all your worries, then this is the best time to weigh the pros and cons. This chapter of the book will help you recognize the advantages and disadvantages of dropshipping so you can consider what you're actually getting into.

Advantages of Dropshipping

1. **Low Overhead** - Once your store is up and running, costs will be quite low. You can even work from a home office to additionally reduce costs. Since you don't claim any stock, you won't have to lease a distribution center space. Being an online store, you likewise needn't bother with a physical space. Your solitary settled expenses are what it takes to run your site, which can be as low as $30 every month. Sweet, right?

2. **Easier To Manage** - Since the dropship providers handle the coordination of delivery and stock, you're able to concentrate all your energy on enhancing the site itself. This gives you more time to deal with other things like marketing, advertising, and ultimately making your customers happy.

3. **Diversification in Products** - Since dropshippers don't have real contact with the items, they're able to offer a more extensive scope of product offerings. This

makes it easy to build a large store relatively quickly, and with low costs associated.

4. **Minimal Investment** - Propelling your own particular dropshipping business requires next to no startup. You can shift your budget to more important things because you don't need to pay for assembling, sending, or lodging stock. Being able to run the business from your laptop also means that you don't need to rent a physical space. Your solitary costs are the expenses of making your site, and any advertising you choose to run.

5. **Extremely Convenient** - The greater part of your work is computerized, so you can operate your business from any place on the planet, and pick your own hours. This also means you can manage your own schedule and don't need to follow a fixed schedule. An absence of stock means you can maintain your business from anyplace with a PC and web connection.

6. **Simple for First Timers** - For somebody who has never made an online store, beginning with drop shipping is genuinely simple. There is very little monetary risk, and so you really have nothing to lose!

Disadvantages of Dropshipping

1. **Trust of Customers** - Like in any business, you must be cautious of whom you join forces with. Some providers are more solid than others, and in the event that you pick the wrong ones, you'll have to deal with more customer issues.

2. **Low Margins** - Not making much per sale is the opposite side of the "low overhead" coin. While some dropshipping businesses have great margins, the majority do not. This greatly depends upon which niche you choose to operate in, as well as what suppliers you work with.

3. **Shipping Challenges and Issues** - Most dropshippers offer items from various providers. In the event that a solitary client purchases items from various providers in a single transaction, the delivery expenses and times will vary.

4. **Unfamiliar Products** - It's a ton simpler to offer an item you've grasped than one you've just seen pictures of. This generally isn't a huge issue however, as you're able to be selective about which items you offer and which you don't.

Chapter 4: Manufacturers vs. Dropship Wholesaler

With all the distinctive terms tossed around in the realm of web based offerings, it can be befuddling what implies what. Regularly the terms are utilized reciprocally, yet they don't mean a similar thing.

At the end of this chapter, you will be able to understand the difference between a manufacturer and a dropship wholesaler to help you decide which one best suits your needs. You basically need to comprehend the three most pertinent players that make up the dropshipping store network: producers, wholesalers and retailers.

Manufacturers – to formally define a manufacturer, they are simply the maker of the item. If by any lucky chance the manufacturer has a dropshipping program in place, this will be the perfect opportunity for you since there is no middle man, meaning that they can give you the best prices. Manufacturers make the item and most don't offer straightforwardly to the general population. Rather, they offer in mass to wholesalers and retailers.

Purchasing directly from the producer is the least expensive approach when buying items for resale; however most won't offer to dropship products.

Wholesalers – these are outsider merchants who purchase products in bulk, directly from the manufacturers. These wholesalers will sometimes sell their products direct to the consumer, as well to other businesses. Wholesalers are much more likely to work with dropshippers, though the margins won't be as good as dealing with manufacturers directly.

Wholesalers will typically stock items from a handful of producers, and have a tendency to work within a particular industry or specialty.

Retailer - A retailer is any individual who offers items directly to the general population at a markup. If you're able to maintain a business by means of dropshipping, then you're a retailer.

A fourth sort of provider is a *"drop transport aggregator"*. A dropship aggregator is a distributer who purchases from huge amounts of various manufacturers to offer you the most stretched out conceivable scope of items from one place.

Chapter 5: Using Shopify for Dropshipping

Shopify, a Canadian web based e-commerce business headquartered in Ottawa, Ontario, was the brainchild of founder Tobias Lütke, Daniel Weinand, and Scott Lake. Estimated to be worth approximately $55 billion in 2017, the company has reported that they are currently engaged with at least 600,000 online traders on a daily basis. Therefore, if one of your questions is why should you partner up with Shopify, then that should answer your question.

To look at the bigger picture, Shopify is the main ecommerce business today, empowering business visionaries and entrepreneurs to begin their online stores with the organization. Because it is incredibly easy to utilize, you'll have the capacity to create your own beautiful and functional store, regardless of whether you have any web design experience or not.

Shopify can easily be used to create a dropshipping website. Uploading product images is simple, and optimizing your website can be done at any time, from practically any web-enabled device.

Here are the simple steps for getting started on Shopify:

1. Register with Shopify

2. Buy Your Web Domain

3. Set Up Email Forwarding

4. Choose a Theme for Your Shopify Store

5. Add Must Have Pages for Drop Shipping

6. Add Products and Brand Collections

7. Add Shopify's Free Customer Review App

8. Pick Your Shopify Plan

9. Finalize Your Shopify Settings

Best Dropshipping Apps that Shopify Offers

Shopify offers many free applications, as well as some paid options. These are usually made by third parties for use on the Shopify platform. These apps can greatly help in running and optimizing your dropshipping store.

Oberlo is an application that has been particularly and solely created for the Shopify platform, and helps business visionaries effectively transfer items specifically to their Shopify store from the AliExpress site or the Oberlo commercial center. By utilizing the Oberlo Shopify dropshipping application you have a whole library of items to look over at– including clothing, gadgets, adornments, toys, and much more. Since Oberlo coordinates specifically with Shopify, the whole procedure of choosing, offering, and sending items is completely mechanized and takes little work on your part.

Modalyst is a great provider of dropshipped items. The items accessible on Modalyst include clothes, shoes, bridal wear, kids' garments, homewares, and more. Modalyst incorporates straightforwardly with your Shopify store so you can include items with only a single click. Modalyst also allows you to oversee orders and which items they have in stock.

Spocket is a Shopify dropshipping application that allows you to work specifically with Etsy merchants. Basically, add the Spocket application to your Shopify store, look through the index of Etsy items, and contact the vender to guarantee you can sell their item on your site. Spocket is right now building up their own particular library of Etsy dealers that have pre-consented to re-offer their items through the Spocket application, which will make sourcing items from Etsy venders considerably less demanding, so watch out for that!

Gooten is a print satisfaction dropshipping administration that gives 100+ curated items to you to browse, include your hand crafts or photographs onto, and afterward have them transported straightforwardly to your clients. They handle the whole assembling, printing, satisfying and delivering process so you don't have to deal with any stock, ever. As far as stock, they stock a wide assortment of kitchen and restroom items, embellishments, home style, photobooks, prints, cards, divider workmanship, attire, pet items and that's only the tip of the iceberg.

Chapter 6: AliExpress Dropshipping

AliExpress, founded in 2010, is an online marketplace made up of independent businesses in China, offering items to worldwide online customers. It is owned by business tycoon Jack Ma's Alibaba. It contains products in almost every category imaginable, most of which are being manufactured in China.

AliExpress is an immense commercial center with a wide variety of items you can offer in your store. Since a large portion of the AliExpress dealers are located in China, their costs are exceptionally competitive.

Numerous venders on AliExpress have awesome photographs for their items that you can use on your site. Finally, dropshipping utilizing AliExpress is as straightforward as requesting the item on AliExpress in the wake of getting a sale, and providing the customer's address. Dropshipping utilizing AliExpress is an incredible method to begin offering a wide variety of products.

As you'll discover with AliExpress, there's a gigantic range of items to browse.

Using AliExpress for Dropshipping

It may be a smart to have an Excel spreadsheet on hand with a rundown of the number of items on your site, the sum you're offering them for, the sum they cost on AliExpress, and a link to the AliExpress page where each particular item is offered. This way, at whatever point you get a sale, it will be less demanding for you to re-discover the seller on AliExpress.

When making a purchase on AliExpress, it's a smart idea to tell the merchant you're dropshipping. Many are familiar with the dropshipping model, and will ensure that the products contain no additional marketing material for their company specifically.

Once everything has been keyed in, you'll get an email in matter of seconds to let you know that your order is confirmed, and you'll be kept in the loop until the item has been delivered and received. The best part about AliExpress dropshipping is that it enables you to rapidly test and approve new items.

Chapter 7: Finding Products to Sell

The greatest obstacle that most dropshippers encounter is picking the items they'd like to sell. The most common error at this stage is picking and item based solely on individual intrigue or enthusiasm.

This is a satisfactory methodology if being keen on the item is your essential goal, but isn't always the best business move. It's key to pick products that a large number of people are interested in, rather than something that has low demand in the marketplace.

How do you make sure your products are actually sustainable? Here are a few tips to ensure the vitality of your online business:

Selecting Products

Here is a list of things to carefully consider when choosing which products you're going to sell:

1. **The Perfect Price** – Make absolutely sure that you can source your product for a good price. Take a look at what the product sells for elsewhere online, and calculate what kind of a profit you'll be able to make per sale. Consider the advertising expense you may have to incur in order to make those sales. If there isn't enough profit left for you at the end of the day, then find another product.

2. **Promotional Potential** – Consider how you will promote and advertise your product. Will you be able to write captivating ad copy? Will you be able to create a viral video ad promoting it? Consider how you can market the product better than the competition carefully.

3. **Elusive Locally** – Selling an item that is elusive locally will expand your odds of success, as long as you don't get excessively particular. This will mean less competition, and a greater share of the market for you!

4. **Guide Pricing** – Some suppliers will set what's known as a base promoted value for their items, and require that all dropshippers and re-sellers value their items at or over a specific level. This price floor stops businesses from selling products at a super low price. This can make it difficult if you were planning to compete on price.

5. **Smaller Is Usually Better** – Generally speaking, smaller products have lower shipping costs. This makes it more viable to ship items farther, without cutting into your margins.

Google Keywords and Search Engine Optimization

The most ideal approach to gauge interest for a thing on the web is to review how many individuals are searching for it, utilizing a web search tool like Google.

Luckily, Google makes this search volume data freely accessible by means of its watchword instrument. Basically type in a word or phrase, and the apparatus reveals to you what numbers of individuals are searching for it on a monthly basis. Make sure that people are actually searching for your particular or product or associated keywords regularly, and in enough volume to make selling it worthwhile.

Conclusion

Once again, thank you for choosing this book on dropshipping. I hope that you now feel comfortable with the idea of dropshipping, and are ready to give this business model a go!

I wish you the best of luck in your entrepreneurial endeavors!

Finally, if you enjoyed this book then please take the time to leave a review on Amazon. Your feedback is greatly appreciated!

www.ingramcontent.com/pod-product-compliance
Lightning Source LLC
LaVergne TN
LVHW020453080526
838202LV00055B/5438